Don't Block the Blessings

How To Keep From
Murmuring and Complaining

by
Robyn Gool

Harrison House
Tulsa, Oklahoma

Unless otherwise indicated, all Scripture quotations are taken from the *King James Version* of the Bible.

Don't Block the Blessings
— *How To Keep From Murmuring and Complaining*
ISBN 0-89274-716-1
Copyright © 1989 by Robyn Gool
P.O. Box 240433
Charlotte, NC 28224

Published by Harrison House, Inc.
P.O. Box 35035
Tulsa, Oklahoma 74153

Contents

Introduction

But with many of them God was not well pleased: for they were overthrown in the wilderness.

Now these things were our examples, to the intent that we should not lust after evil things, as they also lusted.

Neither be ye idolaters, as were some of them; as it is written, The people sat down to eat and drink, and rose up to play.

Neither let us commit fornication, as some of them committed, and fell in one day three and twenty thousand.

Neither let us tempt Christ, as some of them also tempted, and were destroyed of serpents.

Neither murmur ye, as some of them also murmured, and were destroyed of the destroyer.

Now all these things happened unto them for ensamples: and they are written for our admonition, upon whom the ends of the world are come.

1 Corinthians 10:5-11

In this passage the Apostle Paul has provided for us several reasons why the majority of Moses' generation never entered the land which had been promised them by God, a land "flowing with milk and honey," a land which contained everything anyone would ever want or need materially or financially.

Deuteronomy 8:7-14 gives us some insight into the abundant blessings the children of Israel were told they would experience once they had arrived in this new land:

For the Lord thy God bringeth thee into a good land, a land of brooks of water, of fountains and depths that spring out of valleys and hills;

A land of wheat, and barley, and vines, and fig trees, and pomegranates; a land of oil olive, and honey;

A land wherein thou shalt eat bread without scarceness, thou shalt not lack any thing in it; a land whose stones are iron, and out of whose hills thou mayest dig brass.

When thou hast eaten and art full, then thou shalt bless the Lord thy God for the good land which he hath given thee.

Beware that thou forget not the Lord thy God, in not keeping his commandments, and his judgments, and his statutes, which I command thee this day:

Lest when thou hast eaten and art full, and hast built goodly houses, and dwelt therein;

And when thy herds and thy flocks multiply, and thy silver and thy gold is multiplied, and all that thou hast is multiplied.

Then thine heart be lifted up, and thou forget the Lord thy God, which brought thee forth....

This passage informs us of what God intended for His people all along, instead of the four hundred years which they had spent in bondage and lack. There is such a land for you and me today, a place in God in which abundant living will be provided. Through Jesus Christ our Lord, God has made available to us "a land of milk and honey," a life in which there is more than enough for our every need.

However, as we see in 1 Corinthians 10:5-11, certain things kept many of the children of Israel from ever reaching their promised land of abundance. Certain things prevented them from enjoying all that God had intended for them. One of the most important of these hindrances was murmuring and complaining.

This area of murmuring and complaining is often overlooked today, yet Satan has been using it to keep many people from appropriating the blessings of God. As Christians, we guard ourselves against so many snares of the devil, but (generally speaking) we have left this door wide open to the enemy.

It is my desire that the lesson presented in this book will help you to get to your "land of milk and honey." God has commanded us not to give place to the devil. (Eph. 4:27.) I strongly and very deeply believe that in the Body of Christ today murmuring and complaining has been an open door for our adversary, just as it was for God's people under the leadership of Moses.

Let's begin our study together, learning how to avoid murmuring and complaining so that we can be champions for Jesus and keep the devil where he belongs — under our feet!

1
Plan Your Day

A lot of our murmuring and complaining is self-induced because of poor planning.

One of the foremost things to be done to eliminate murmuring and complaining is to plan and schedule your day ahead of time. Think it through before it begins. Don't just get up and get going; prepare yourself spiritually, mentally and physically by outlining your day's activities. Get an overview of your day before it starts. Make time projections and allotments. This can be done at the beginning of the week, the night before, or the morning of your day. But whenever you choose — do it!

Plan your day!

In Mark 1:35-38 we see Jesus (Who is our example) after a full day and evening of ministry getting up before dawn to pray and plan His new day. Read this passage. Great miracles and deliverances had taken place the day before, and the whole city had come out seeking Him. Even Peter desired Jesus to minister to the people. However, Jesus had His direction. He had already planned His day. So He announced that it was time for Him to move on to another mission field.

If you don't plan your day, others will plan and schedule it for you. That always produces frustration, murmuring and complaining.

Proverbs 24:27 tells us: **Prepare thy work without, and make it fit for thyself in the field; and afterwards build thine house.** In Luke 14:28-32 Jesus talks about the importance of planning before going to war or starting to build. Solomon says that the prudent man foresees evil and avoids it. (Prov. 22:3; 27:12.)

God wants us to plan and schedule our day, our time and our lives.

A word of warning and caution needs to be injected here. Avoid becoming legalistic and bound by your schedule. How do you do that? By allowing room *mentally* for interruptions. In the normal course of the day, there will be interruptions as you pursue your plans. However, if you have prepared mentally, that preparation will keep you from murmuring and complaining.

Remember the account of Jairus in Mark 5. His daughter was at the point of death, and Jesus agreed to come and lay His hands on her so she could live. On the way to Jairus' house, a woman full of faith touches Jesus' clothes and is healed of her infirmity. Jesus takes time to stop and listen to her testimony. I imagine Jairus was steaming inside and thinking to himself, "Come on, Jesus; let's go — my daughter is on her death bed!" But even when word came that the young girl had already died, Jesus was in total control of that situation and told Jairus to just keep on believing. End result: Jairus' daughter was healed.

The point is that Jesus was flexible. He allowed for interruptions in His plans. He continued to function without becoming frustrated or distressed. As you and I keep our faith in God, as we keep on believing, interruptions can come and we won't react by murmuring or complaining. Like Jairus, we will still receive our miracle.

As you plan your day, remain open to alterations. Determine to be flexible, if the need arises. The Bible teaches us not to say that tomorrow we are going to do this and go there, but to say, "If the Lord wills." (James 4:13-15.) So plan your day and then follow your plan, but if your schedule is somehow disrupted and your activities curtailed, say,

"Lord, You are my God, and I know that You will see to it that everything works out fine."

I am not saying to believe God *for* interruptions, but simply to realize that interruptions can and do occur. Be prepared mentally in advance, and you will be able to say with Paul, **...none of these things move me...**(Acts 20:24). If you are not prepared mentally, continued frustration will set in. You will push your body to the limit trying to get everything done in spite of the interruptions. The end result will be murmuring and complaining.

That's why you should plan your day. Then the *most important* projects or activities will have priority, and the major tasks will be accomplished each day. *Every* goal of *each* day will not be achieved on the *same* day. Take the pressure off yourself!

Proper planning of each day helps to shut the door on the devil. Remember how Jesus prepared for the Passover ahead of time? He sent two disciples ahead of the team to prepare the upper room for their Passover meal. (Luke 22:7-13.) He was thinking ahead. Remember also what He did when the time had come for Him to enter Jerusalem and give His life for us? He sent disciples ahead to bring back the colt on which He would make His triumphal entry into the city. (Luke 19:28-40.)

Many of us are murmuring and complaining because instead of going after life and laying hold of it, we simply sit back and allow it to come to us. We need to plan our life as well as our day.

Everything that happens to us is not the will of God, nor is it always the devil's fault when things go wrong. We should endeavor to be more flexible and make allowances for changes in plans because of unforeseen circumstances.

For example, suppose you usually have dinner at six o'clock in the evening but today you see that you are going to be late getting home and preparing the elaborate meal

11

you had planned. This is the time to be flexible about altering your dinner menu. A simple, easier-to-prepare meal will be just as satisfying and appreciated. Oftentimes running home and trying to do all that cooking anyway only leads to a miserable evening — and murmuring and complaining.

This concept of flexible planning applies to every area of our lives. It will produce joy and peace of mind every time.

2

Take Time to Rest

We live in a world in which everybody is in a hurry. We are known as "the jet set society"; everyone is on the move, seldom slowing down or taking time to rest. The sad part of all this is that many of those who are in such a hurry don't even know where they are going.

In Romans 12:2, the Spirit of God exhorts us, **...be not conformed to this world, but be ye transformed by the renewing of your mind, that ye may prove what is that good, and acceptable, and perfect, will of God.** I believe the perfect will of God is that we rest — which is the second key to our victory over murmuring and complaining.

> **And the apostles gathered themselves together unto Jesus, and told him all things, both what they had done, and what they had taught.**
>
> **And he said unto them, Come ye yourselves apart into a desert place, and rest a while: for there were many coming and going, and they had no leisure so much as to eat.**
>
> **Mark 6:30,31**

In this passage we see that Jesus knew the importance of rest. Oftentimes He would go into a desert place or a mountain area to rest and pray. This valuable lesson is being imparted to His disciples and must be grasped by all believers today.

To overcome murmuring and complaining, to defeat the devil in our lives, we must be refreshed — in spirit, soul and body. When human beings are weary physically, they are affected mentally and emotionally. When we are affected emotionally, we look at things differently. Our perspectives and attitude change. However, when we're fresh physically, we feel better mentally, and our thinking is clearer and sharper.

When we are physically tired, things always look much worse than they really are. The challenges and obstacles of life seem insurmountable, things and people aggravate and irritate us, and murmuring and complaining begin to surface. God wants us to rest and keep our total being fresh.

Did you notice that Jesus took His disciples apart so they couldn't be disturbed? No matter who we are, we too need rest without disturbance.

I encourage you to deliberately, purposefully, set periods of time in your schedule for rest. Allow time to refresh yourself: spirit, soul and body. The Bible tells us: **...they that wait upon the Lord shall renew their strength; they shall mount up with wings as eagles; they shall run, and not be weary; and they shall walk, and not faint** (Is. 40:31). Let me ask you a question. How can you wait on the Lord if you are constantly answering the phone while you are supposed to be resting, praying, reading the Bible or worshipping God? To wait on the Lord, you need undisturbed peace and quietness.

Once you have located a time to take a nap, meditate on the Word of God, or just relax, purpose in your heart that you will not allow yourself to be disturbed by answering the phone or talking to anyone. If you do answer the phone or go to the door, tell the person — no matter who it is: mother, father, grandfather, whoever — that you are not able to talk right then but that you will contact him or her later. You can always return a call or a visit. If you have an answering machine on your telephone, use it. Never forget that if you don't control your time, other people will.

The "bottom line" is — get some rest.

In 1 Thessalonians 5:23, the Apostle Paul writes: **...I pray God your whole spirit and soul and body be preserved**

blameless unto the coming of our Lord Jesus Christ. Your physical body needs rest. Your mind needs refreshing. Your spirit needs to stay strong. All three must be strengthened and renewed. And that demands time — undisturbed time.

There is nothing wrong with ministering to yourself. That is not being selfish; it's being like God. After spending six days creating the heavens and the earth, our Creator rested (ceased all work) on the seventh day and ordained rest for all of His creation. He established a time of rest for the land itself from producing crops, and He saw to it that His people had a period of rest from work and war. He set the earth in motion in such a way that there would be day and night — a time for activity and a time for sleep.

Did you know that this world is going to keep on going even if you are not around? Did you know that you can do more for God when you take time to rest for thirty minutes to an hour daily than you can by pushing yourself the whole day long? Every part of you (spirit, soul and body) will rise to the challenges of the day more effectively.

Let's enjoy rest and *longevity,* rather than experiencing weariness and burnout. Let's have joy instead of murmuring and complaining.

Take time daily to pray and worship God. Take time daily to read and meditate on the Word of God. But also (and this is almost blanketly ignored) *endeavor* to take time daily to rest your body.

Every year we take a vacation from our job for a period of one to four weeks. Why not take a "mini-vacation" every day for thirty minutes to an hour? Let's learn to slow ourselves down, relax and come back strong, accomplishing more for God with the Spirit of Jesus and the fruit of the Spirit — and with the devil under our feet!

3

Remember That Nothing
Is as Big as It Seems

With God on your side, nothing is as big as it seems. If you can get that truth firmly imbedded in your spirit, then you will not allow yourself to become disheartened, overwhelmed or defeated by the adverse circumstances of life. It is only when you let things become magnified in your mind (forgetting that if God be for you, who can be against you) that you have a tendency to murmur and complain.

For an example, let's consider the feeding of the multitude. (Mark 8:1-9.)

In essence, Jesus said to His disciples, "These people have been with me for three days and I don't want to send them away hungry lest they faint on their journey and die of starvation. Give them something to eat."

His disciples answered: "What? How are we going to feed all these people?" They reacted just as we have done in times past. They forgot Who they were with.

With God nothing is as big as it seems. The situation seemed so overpowering to the disciples. So before murmuring could start, Jesus asked them, "How many loaves do you have?" Taking the loaves and the few fish they had, He blessed them and ordered that they be distributed to the people. The result was that everyone had enough to eat, and several basketsful of food were gathered up.

Jesus did not despair or become distraught in the face of a seemingly impossible situation. As His disciples, neither should we.

It is the devil's job to amplify and magnify the negative aspects of life, to blow them out of proportion and make us think there is no way over the obstacles placed in our path. That is one way he gets us to murmur and complain.

When faced with adverse circumstances or obstacles, we must learn to say: "I have God on my side; He is with me. The Bible says that nothing is impossible or too hard for God. With His help I *will* overcome!"

> And say thou unto the people, Sanctify yourselves against to morrow, and ye shall eat flesh: for ye have wept in the ears of the Lord, saying, Who shall give us flesh to eat? for it was well with us in Egypt: therefore the Lord will give you flesh, and ye shall eat.
>
> Ye shall not eat one day, nor two days, nor five days, neither ten days, nor twenty days;
>
> But even a whole month, until it come out at your nostrils, and it be loathsome unto you: because that ye have despised the Lord which is among you, and have wept before him, saying, Why came we forth out of Egypt?
>
> And Moses said, The people, among whom I am, are six hundred thousand footmen; and thou hast said, I will give them flesh, that they may eat a whole month.
>
> Shall the flocks and the herds be slain for them, to suffice them? or shall all the fish of the sea be gathered together for them, to suffice them?
>
> And the Lord said unto Moses, Is the Lord's hand waxed short? thou shalt see now whether my word shall come to pass unto thee or not....
>
> And there went forth a wind from the Lord, and brought quails from the sea, and let them fly by the camp, as it were a day's journey on this side, and as it were a day's journey on the other side, round about the camp, as it were two cubits high upon the face of the earth.
>
> **Numbers 11:18-23,31**

In this passage we see how the people murmured and complained that they had no "flesh" (meat) to eat. So the Lord commanded Moses to tell them that they would eat meat for a whole month, until they were sick of it. The Lord rebuked Moses for not believing that He was able to fulfill His promise to supply food for the children of Israel — which He did in abundance. (v. 31.) God watches over His Word to perform it!

On another occasion, the king of Israel and his fighting men ran out of water for themselves and their animals. There seemed no way they could survive the desert, much less overcome their enemy, the Moabites. But notice what the Lord said through Elisha His prophet:

> And he said, Thus saith the Lord, Make this valley full of ditches.
>
> For thus saith the Lord, Ye shall not see wind, neither shall ye see rain; yet that valley shall be filled with water, that ye may drink, both ye, and your cattle, and your beasts.
>
> And *this is but a light thing in the sight of the Lord:* he will deliver the Moabites also into your hand.
>
> 2 Kings 3:16-18

In that same chapter we read the conclusion of the story:

> And it came to pass, in the morning, when the meat offering was offered, that, behold, there came water by the way of Edom, and the country was filled with water....
>
> And when they came to the camp of Israel, the Israelites rose up and smote the Moabites, so that they fled before them....
>
> 2 Kings 3:20,24

God kept His Word; He supplied the needs of His people and gave them victory over their enemies. Nothing is too hard for our heavenly Father, and He is on our side — as the psalmist wrote: **The Lord is on my side; I will not fear: what can man do unto me?** (Ps. 118:6). The prophet Isaiah decreed, **No weapon that is formed against thee shall prosper...**(Is. 54:17). Jesus proclaimed that the gates of hell shall not prevail against His Church. (Matt. 16:18.) That means that every born-again, blood-bought, blood-washed individual on earth can have an assurance of victory. Jesus has overcome the world, and His victory is our victory. (John 16:33.) Let's keep that truth in our consciousness.

The devil will try to make you think that your financial picture is so devastating that there is no way you can ever get out of it. He will tell you that you're going under, you're losing your house, your car and everything you own. That's the time to stand up and declare: "Nothing is as big as it seems because I have God on my side. He will deliver me because He supplies all of my needs according to His riches in glory by Christ Jesus. I am the head and not the tail; I am blessed coming in and going out; I have been delivered from the power of darkness and redeemed from the curse of the law." (Ps. 118:6; Phil. 4:19; Deut. 28:13,6; Col. 1:13; Gal. 3:13.)

Talk to yourself and let the Word you confess get into your spirit. When it does, it will begin to transform your mind and help you to be slow to speak. (James 1:19.) Then, when you do speak, what you say will be consistent with the Word of God — not murmuring and complaining.

Nothing is a as big as the devil tries to make it appear — not when you belong to God. Whenever Satan moves in to discourage you, remind yourself that the weapons of your warfare are not carnal, but mighty through God to the pulling down of strongholds. (2 Cor. 10:4.) Talk to yourself. Never allow self to talk to you without talking back. If you listen to your own fears and self-pity, they will produce murmuring, complaining and discouragement — one hundred percent of the time.

A great example of this truth is found in 1 Samuel 30:1-6. Read this passage in your rest time. You will see how David and his men returned to their city to find it in ashes and all their loved ones taken captive. Those under David's command began to murmur and complain; they even considered stoning David. But the Bible says that David encouraged *himself* in the Lord. (v. 6.) Self was talking and

David had to talk back. I believe this self-talk by David is the basis of Psalms 42 and 103.

Remember: never let self talk to you without talking back. To do so is to give place to the devil. (Eph. 4:27.) It produces murmuring and complaining. Nothing is as big as it seems when you have God.

4

Realize That God Is With You

Realize that God is with you in everything. No matter what your situation in life, He is there with you. You are not alone. God is going through your trials with you. If you can remember that vital truth, it will keep you from murmuring and complaining.

> **Let your conversation be without covetousness; and be content with such things as ye have: for he hath said, I will never leave thee nor forsake thee.**
>
> **So that we may boldly say, The Lord is my helper, and I will not fear what man shall do unto me.**
>
> **Hebrews 13:5,6**

Do you see why we can be content? Because God has said that He will never leave us nor forsake us. That being true, we don't have to "lose our cool." We don't have to panic, weep, or lose sleep at night. We don't have to murmur, complain, become judgmental or give up and "throw in the towel."

In Isaiah 43:2 the Lord tells us: **When thou passest through the waters, I will be with thee; and through the rivers, they shall not overflow thee: when thou walkest through the fire, thou shalt not be burned; neither shall the flame kindle upon thee.** This scripture should be enough to keep us from murmuring and complaining.

In Hebrews 13:5 the writer exhorts us, "Let your conversation be without covetousness...." Do you know what murmuring is? It's a form of covetousness. Think about it for a moment. When we murmur and complain, we are coveting a particular situation or change in circumstance: "I wish I weren't going through this; why do I have to be in this predicament?" Instead, we ought to be saying, "Jesus, You are with me and all things are subject to change and are already in the process of changing. Thanks be unto God Who always causes me to triumph in Christ Jesus." (2 Cor. 2:14.) That's a totally different atmosphere.

The writer of Hebrews also tells us, ". . .and be content with such things as ye have: for he hath said, I will never leave thee, nor forsake thee." Whatever situation in which we find ourselves, we can be like Paul who said in essence, "I have learned to be content in any condition because, whether I am abased or abound, I know that my God is there with me." (Phil. 4:11).

"So that we may boldly say, The Lord is my helper, and I will not fear what man shall do unto me." The believer can boldly say that, because we know that God never leaves us nor forsakes us, that He is our helper and we are going to come out of the situation. The storm will cease its raging and the water will be stilled. So there is no sense in murmuring and complaining. There is no need to get "bent out of shape," because we are going to come through victoriously.

Realize that God is with you in everything. That is one of the greatest lessons that God is endeavoring to get across to His Body, the Church.

I can remember when, due to an NCAA technicality, I lost my athletic scholarship during my senior year at Oral Roberts University. I was walking across the campus with tears rolling down my face and saying, "I'm going to quit school and get a job." This was in the middle of my murmuring and complaining about the situation.

Suddenly I heard the Lord speak on the inside of me: "I want to teach you something now. Never make an institution your source. I am your Source." At that time I was married and was depending upon the scholarship stipend for income. When I said, "Okay, Lord, I see it and repent," He turned that situation around. In just a few days I was awarded another scholarship that gave me the freedom to work and produce income for my family (which is not allowed on an athletic scholarship).

God was there for me, and He is there for you right now. He is always there. The sooner we realize this truth, the faster we will experience victory over murmuring and complaining.

5
Realize That Obstacles Will Come

Realize that there will be obstacles and struggles in this life. If you will accept this world as real, and not act as though being a Christian should merit your living in an ivory tower, a bubble of immunity, then you will be less likely to murmur and complain when things go wrong. When you are spiritually alert, you understand that struggles will come. Obstacles will present themselves. The devil will see to that. But, if you try to live with your head in the sky as if Christians are not supposed to have problems, then when troubles do come your way, you will murmur and complain.

Jesus put it this way: **...In the world ye shall have tribulation: but be of good cheer; I have overcome the world** (John 16:33).

I never get up in the morning expecting trouble, but I always keep the attitude that if trouble comes, I'll be ready for it. I remind myself that as a Christian I belong to God, I'm the righteousness of Christ, the salt of the earth, the light of the world, more than a conqueror — and this world belongs to Satan. He is not my lord, so if there is anybody he is out to hurt, it is me. Therefore, if trouble comes my way, I remember to be sober and to resist the devil. (1 Pet. 5:8,9.) I realize that because I am born again, going upstream in a seemingly downstream world, struggles, oppositions and persecutions will come my way. Challenges will come.

The only way to avoid them is to go home to be with the Lord. But there is no need to do that; He is coming back for us. Until then, I'll just demonstrate Satan's defeat through my big Brother, Jesus Christ!

I don't have my faith out looking for trouble. Nor am I am like some Christians who think they are immune to hardship once they get saved. No, that's a pitfall; it causes great harm to believers. We are in a real world, with ungodly people who are influenced by the devil to do ungodly things. There is a warfare going on in the realm of the spirit. But the good news is that we are on the winning side. We can live triumphantly through the blood of Jesus. We overcome by the blood of the Lamb and the word of our testimony. (Rev. 12:11.) I testify that Satan is defeated and that Jesus is Lord; therefore, I don't need to murmur and complain.

In Philippians 2:14,15 Paul says in essence, "Sons of God don't complain." Why should we? Jesus is Lord!

No, I don't wake up in the morning saying, "Father, give me trouble today." But I do realize that life is real and that there is going to be some ugly situations to deal with in my lifetime.

Recently our church finished building a three-million-dollar facility. The building was erected debt-free, but in the process some devastating circumstances arose. We were challenged by a lack of funds; getting specific colors, materials and designs; obtaining city sewer service; receiving our occupancy permit (to name a few). However, instead of murmuring and complaining, we spoke to the problem. The church came together and held a praise service, and the hand of God began to move. We saw God supply finances, give us favor, turn situations around, and move us in right on time. Hallelujah! We stilled our enemy with praise as God inhabits the praises of His people. (Ps. 22:3.)

There is a mind set which believers must have. We are in this world, but not of it. When we get to heaven, there won't be any more tears, sorrows or troubles. But we are in this world right now, and until we are out of it we need to have our minds fixed on the Word of God so when trials and tests come, we will take that Word and overcome them in the name of Jesus. Let's use the Word, the name of Jesus, intercessory prayer, praise, faith and the power of God to overcome the devil — because greater is He that is in us than he that is in the world. (1 John 4:4.)

I was out of the country recently as part of a mission team which went into Russia and Finland. When we arrived, everybody's luggage showed up but mine. That's a great opportunity to murmur and complain. Instead I decided to keep my mind on Kingdom business and ignore the devil. I wanted God to use me. I went five days without a change of clothes and with no opportunity to buy any. The ministry team was kind, offering me articles of clothing and anything else I could use.

The devil wanted me to complain, but I wanted the anointing. When my opportunity came to minister the Word, over one hundred people were filled with the Holy Ghost, and many gave their hearts to Jesus. That could not have happened if I had been murmuring every day, in every church service, about not having proper clothing for the meetings. When we prayed for the sick, there were many wonderful healings and deliverances. It was great to be a part of the flow of God and not give the devil place.

Challenges will come, but Jesus is Lord!

6

Submit Your Tongue to God

This is the last point in our discussion, but perhaps it is the most important of them all. In order to avoid murmuring and complaining, we must submit our tongue to the power of the Holy Ghost.

> My brethren, be not many masters, knowing that we shall receive the greater condemnation.
>
> For in many things we offend all. If any man offend not in word, the same is a perfect man, and able also to bridle the whole body.
>
> Behold, we put bits in the horses' mouths, that they may obey us; and we turn about their whole body.
>
> Behold also the ships, which though they be so great, and are driven of fierce winds, yet are they turned about with a very small helm, whithersoever the governor listeth.
>
> Even so the tongue is a little member, and boasteth great things. Behold, how great a matter a little fire kindleth!
>
> And the tongue is a fire, a world of iniquity: so is the tongue among our members, that it defileth the whole body, and setteth on fire the course of nature; and it is set on fire of hell.
>
> For every kind of beasts, and of birds, and of serpents, and of things in the sea, is tamed, and hath been tamed of mankind:
>
> But the tongue can no man tame; it is an unruly evil, full of deadly poison.
>
> James 3:1-8

Remember this truth and never forget it. You cannot tame your tongue by yourself. However, you can submit your tongue to God and ask Him to put a bridle on it and a guard over your mouth. Ask Him to cause your speech to be always with grace and to help you watch over the words you speak. (Col. 4:6.) Say to God, "Lord, I submit my tongue to You. I invite You to discipline my tongue, my language, my mouth, my words, my speech."

Now you may think this is impossible because you simply haven't been able to control your tongue. It may be impossible for you, but with God all things are possible. (Matt. 19:26.) You don't have to give up or become discouraged about the words that you speak.* God wants your tongue trained. He loves you, and as you yield your tongue to Him daily, and cooperate with Him, He will begin to tame your unruly tongue. Your days of murmuring and complaining will come to an end, and in all things you will be giving thanks, ...for this is is the will of God in Christ Jesus concerning you (1 Thess. 5:18).

---

*There are several books by Charles Capps and Kenneth Hagin on the subject of the tongue and the power of words which will be of great value for further study.